Melons at the Parsonage

A Play

Nick Warburton

A SAMUEL FRENCH ACTING EDITION

SAMUEL FRENCH

FOUNDED 1830

SAMUELFRENCH-LONDON.CO.UK
SAMUELFRENCH.COM

FOR AMATEUR PRODUCTION ENQUIRIES

UNITED KINGDOM AND WORLD
EXCLUDING NORTH AMERICA

plays@SamuelFrench-London.co.uk

020 7255 4302/01

Each title is subject to availability from Samuel French,

depending upon country of performance.

CHARACTERS

Ted, adjudicator
Iris, Chairperson
The Bletchworth Players:
      Vicar (male if possible)
      Maid (female)
      Spinster
Frantic Jam:
      One
      Two
      Three (female)
Stage Manager

The cast should be augmented by extra members of the two teams, supporters of each group, trophy collectors, etc.

The action of the play takes place on a stage of a hall

Time: the present

Melons at the Parsonage was first performed at Stapleford, Cambridgeshire, on 19th February, 1999, with the following cast:

Leanne Betts, Naomi Bryant, Guy Chisholm, Katy Farmer, Jo Jewel, Jamie Newman, Stephanie Newman, Janet Phipps, Rose Robinson, Claire Watkins and Meghan Warth.

The play was directed by Jean Green and Carol Tomson

Other plays by Nick Warburton published by
Samuel French Ltd

Distracted Globe
Domby-Dom
Don't Blame It On the Boots
Droitwich Discovery
Easy Stages
The Last Bread Pudding
The Loophole
Not Bobby
Office Song
Receive This Light
Round the World With Class 6
Sour Grapes and Ashes
Zartan

PRODUCTION NOTES

Melons at the Parsonage can be played by adult or youth groups. Or mixed, I suppose: it might be interesting to have Bletchworth played by adults and Frantic Jam by young actors. Certain script changes may be necessary, depending on casting. For example, Iris is described in her role as "tall and willowy"; if the actress playing her *is* tall and willowy, change the line (to "elfin and petite" or something). The point is that she has obviously been miscast. She's the wrong size, shape and age—but she still gets the prize! The members of the two groups speak in two voices—their own, natural voice for exchanges with Ted etc., and a completely different voice for when they are performing. Bletchworth speak in rough London or thick regional accents, but become extremely refined when acting. It's the other way round for Frantic Jam. Their natural speech is refined and "proper", but they affect coarse accents for their performance.

N. W.

MELONS AT THE PARSONAGE

The stage of a hall, set for the Awards Presentation after a drama festival

The CURTAINS *open on the adjudicator, Ted, and the chairperson, Iris. Ted is sitting with his clipboard on his knee by a table. On the table are a large white cloth bearing the legend "BOGOFF", a large tasteless trophy, several tiny trophies, a jug of water and a glass. Iris is standing ready to address the audience, among whom are planted various supporters of the groups*

Iris Ladies and gentlemen, we come now to the moment you've all been waiting for—the results of the twenty-sixth Barnley Operatic Group's Festival Fair—and it's my very great pleasure to introduce to you the man whose wit and insight has entertained us over the past ten days and forty plays...

Ted stands and strides forward

He is, of course, an actor himself, well-known for his ability to produce both tears and laughter, and for his impeccable timing...

Ted backs away and sits again

...Mr Ted Withers!

Ted stands again

Needless to say, we hope that Ted will produce not too many tears of disappointment tonight...

Ted sits again and Iris laughs alone at her own joke

...but rather the laughter of success for the winning group. (*Firmly*) In which we will all share. A healthy debate over theatrical niceties is all very well but it should stop well short of beating up the adjudicator in the bike sheds after the festival. You will notice, by the way, that BOGOFF has *not* invited back the Crimley Townswomen's Guild this year. Well, I'm sure you don't want to listen to me all evening...

Voice From The Audience Hear, hear!

Iris (*with a frosty glare at the audience*) ...so let me hand over without further ado to Ted Withers!

Ted hesitates, crouching

Mr Ted Withers!

Ted jumps up and comes forward with his clipboard

Ted Thank you, Iris. It's a real treat for me to be asked to BOGOFF this year. Well, four plays a night for ten solid days. How entertained we've all been! Let me begin by saying a few words about each of them...

As he thumbs through his notes, there is a groan from the audience. Iris leaps up and whispers in his ear

(*To Iris*) What?

She whispers fiercely

(*To the audience*) So—straight on with the awards, then. The Arthur Adams Construction Company Trophy for the best set goes, for their splendid creation of a Dogger Bank trawler, to ... the Dashford Modellers.

A smattering of applause

An ecstatic person in a DJ and a cloth cap comes up to collect one of the tiny trophies. As he (or she) goes off to muted applause...

In fact, their new play, *Haddock*, might've featured in the main awards, had they got their boat on and off with a little more urgency. The four minutes we did see, though, were, I think you'll all agree, most impressive. And now the Toby Burk-Spilling Cup to the best actor. This goes to one of the most convincing performances of a shambling drunk I have ever seen. He was embarrassing, he was loud and unpleasant, and he fell off the stage as if he'd been doing it all his life. The Barnley Best Actor for this year is ... George Pelham!

A smattering of applause. No sign of George

Are you there, George?
Voice From The Audience He's down the pub!
Ted In that case, we shall move on to the Gloria Stenhouse Trophy for Best Actress. For her performance as the tall and willowy waif in *My Doctor, My Lover*, our best actress is ... Iris Cowley!

Iris looks shocked and pleased as she collects her trophy. A smattering of applause

Voice From The Audience Not again!
Ted And now, in reverse order, the top three plays. Third, a haunting piece about the passion of a tall and willowy waif for her Polish doctor... The Barnley Operatic Group for *My Doctor, My Lover*!

A smattering of applause. Cries of "Fix!". Iris glowers, then collects the trophy

And second? Well, there was no second.

A gasp from the audience

Joint winners of this year's Barnley Freepress Echo Trophy
were... The Bletchworth Players in *A Killing at the Parsonage*
and Frantic Jam Experimental Theatre in *To Make Do With
Melons*!

Applause from various supporters

*Some of the Bletchworth group come up in costume—a Vicar, a
Maid and an elderly Spinster—followed by some from Frantic
Jam, all in black tights, white gloves and leotards*

*There is some jostling with the huge trophy as each group tries to
claim it. Iris steps forward*

Iris Will you stop tugging it?

Cowed by Iris, the groups shrink back

Those handles are only plastic, you know. Thank you. (*To the
audience*) Ladies and gentlemen, as you are no doubt all aware,
the constitution of BOGOFF won't allow joint winners, so we
have to apply rule six sub-clause four b in order to separate the
teams...
Vicar Why don't we simply put it to the audience?
Ted Oh, I hardly think so...
Vicar Ask them whether they preferred a neat little mystery with
a proper story, or a hotchpotch of pretentious poncing about by
a——
Jam 1 I say! Just because you didn't understand it——
Vicar Nobody understood it, mate.
Ted I did...
Jam 2 Thank you. I said he was brighter than he looked, didn't I?
Ted ...up to a point.
Maid I think Anthony's right, though. If we ask the audience——
Ted We can't ask them. They're not trained.
Iris No, no. Rule six sub-clause four b clearly states that in the case
of a dead heat there will have to be a play-off.

Jam 3 You've just made that up.
Vicar We're not having a play-off. Ask the audience...
Jam 2 No!
Ted (*calming them*) Listen to me, all of you. We have to settle this
one way or the other, so we'll go ahead with the play-off...
Spinster Pathetic!
Ted ...unless one of you wants to concede.

Cries of "Never!" and "You must be joking!" which again he quells

Well, if you won't concede, and you won't take part in a play-off,
I shall have to award the cup to The Barnley Operatic Group.
Iris (*snatching the cup*) As you should've done in the first place.
Jam 1 (*snatching it back*) No, no. We're not having that.
Maid Award it to a willowy waif who looks more like a brick
privvie?
Ted (*snatching the trophy and putting it on the table*) In that case—
ladies and gentlemen, an added bonus for you all. Another thirty
minutes of cracking theatre.

Groans all round

Frantic Jam versus The Bletchworth Players. Head to head.
Stewards, lock those doors. No-one is leaving till we've got a
winner! What happens next, Iris?
Iris It's in the rules. Each team performs a scene from their own play
and a scene from the other—and you judge on that.
Ted Very well, then. Clear the stage for The Bletchworth Players
in a scene from *A Killing at the Parsonage*.

A stage manager, looking extremely fed-up, comes on to supervise

*The Vicar and the Spinster exit while the others stand aside to
watch*

*The Lights dip. There is music—something tuneful and jolly English.
As it fades, the Maid takes centre stage and the Lights come up*

brightly. There is birdsong. The following scene is an odd mix of melodramatic posturing and wooden delivery. The Maid sings tunelessly to herself as she polishes the trophies. From time to time she looks round to make sure the Vicar is coming

> *The Vicar enters with exaggerated furtiveness and stands behind her. He coughs and she gives a little jump*

Maid Oh! Bless me, Vicar, I did not see you there!

Vicar You're looking in fine fettle today, Jasmine.

Maid (*blushing and confused*) Oh, sir, you must not be so familiar. Miss Littlewood, the mistress of the house, may come upon us at any moment.

Vicar I don't care, I tell you.

Maid But surely you remember that you are engaged to Miss Littlewood, and that she is a woman who, though handsome and much-admired, has saved herself for the time when you can be married?

Vicar Yes, Jasmine, I know. Oh, curse the day I allowed her to play fast and loose with my unknowing heart!

Maid But for the objection of her brother, Colonel Littlewood, late of India, you would be married even now.

Vicar Yes, yes. And yet if we married, the Colonel would cut her out of his will because of his strange aversion to clergymen. We would be penniless.

Maid I am already penniless, Hector.

Vicar Oh, Jasmine! If only the Littlewoods would disappear, leaving their wealth behind, then you and I...

Maid Oh, Hector!

Vicar Oh, Jasmine!

They look nervously around and then go into a clinch

> *The Spinster enters and recoils with shock*

They see her. The Maid polishes furiously and the Vicar ties his shoelace

Spinster Hector! What is the meaning of this?

Vicar Things are not as they seem, Henrietta. Your brother, the Colonel, asked me to speak to your maid here, to comfort her in her sadness...

Spinster Indeed?

Maid Yes, ma'am. Begging your pardon, ma'am. The Vicar was consoling me. You see, my poor aunt has gone down with the malaria again.

Spinster (*thrown*) Malaria?

Maid Yes.

Spinster Malaria?

Maid No. Not malaria... (*She's forgotten the line*) She's gone down with ... with...

Jam 1 (*jumping up*) Prompt! They need a prompt!

Maid She's gone down with ... with...

Ted leaps forward with his clipboard, rather like a boxing referee. He begins to count her out

Ted One ... two ... three...

The Jam contingent chant "Prompt! Prompt!"

Vicar Was it not the lumbago, my dear?

Maid (*in her own voice*) No, no. It was something else...

Vicar I believe it was the lumbago.

Spinster Yes, it was the lumbago. (*Aside, in her own voice*) Just get on with it.

Maid That's right, the lumbago.

Jam 2 She fluffed, she fluffed! Deduct a point!

Vicar (*threatening, in his own voice*) You watch yourself, mush, or I'll...

Jam 2 He's changing the script. He should be disqualified!

Spinster (*pressing on*) I am not at all convinced by this talk of fever... I mean lumbago. But I cannot deal with this now. I have just come from the conservatory. The Colonel is ... is...

Jam 3 Prompt! Another prompt!
Spinster (*in her own voice*) That was a dramatic pause, you plonker! (*She resumes*) The Colonel is … dead!

They all strike a dramatic attitude of shock and horror. The Maid faints and the Vicar catches her. The Lights fade and the jolly English music returns. The Lights return to normal and they bow deeply. Applause, led heartily by their supporters

Ted (*coming forward*) Thank you, thank you. And now to adjudicate that scene…
Iris We haven't got time for that. Just give the marks.
Ted Oh, all right, then. Seven and a half out of ten.
Vicar Seven and an 'alf! Why only seven and an 'alf?
Ted Well, it was slightly disjointed and you took a prompt.
Vicar (*to the Maid*) You dozy cow!

Bletchworth stalk to the sidelines, muttering

Ted And now a scene from Frantic Jam in *To Make Do With Melons*!

The miserable stage manager returns and makes some signals

The Lights go down. Weird electronic music is heard

As the music fades, red and green lights come up (possibly throbbing) and Frantic Jam are discovered in bizarre, angular positions. One holds a cymbal. Pause

Spinster Prompt! Prompt!
Jam 2 (*in own voice*) Get stuffed. We haven't started yet.

The cymbal is struck

Jam 1 (*resonantly*) The rats are gnawing at the skirting board!

Frantic Jam The rats! The rats!

A rolling note on the cymbal and they writhe sensuously about

Jam 2 Father of rats, speak to us! Leave the broken bedstead and the curled remains of last night's sandwiches! The blood of the questing rat has entered our veins!
Jam 3 We scuttle in shadows!
Frantic Jam Scuttle, scuttle, scuttle...
Jam 1 We scavenge and seek!
Frantic Jam We become rats in your name!
Vicar What a load of rubbish.
Jam 1 (*in own voice, to Ted*) Are you going to stop him chipping in? Because I refuse to practise my art if some Philistine is...
Vicar Your *art*? Don't make me laugh.
Jam 1 ...if some half-baked Philistine is going to mock.
Ted Bletchworth, you are warned. Keep quiet while these good people perform.
Vicar While they ponce about wasting our time, you mean.
Ted That's it! Half a point deducted from Bletchworth!
Vicar 'Alf a point! You buffoon...

But the Maid and the Spinster drag him back and silence him

Ted Proceed.

A bang on the cymbal. Frantic Jam writhe about again

Frantic Jam The blood of the rat! The blood of the rat! (*Etc.*)

Jam 3 slinks over to Ted and runs her fingers through his hair and over his chest

Jam 3 The blood of the rat courses through my veins!
Spinster Bloomin' disgusting.

A rolling note on the cymbal. They all run C *and form an artistic huddle. Pause. The red and green lights fade and the weird music comes up. End music. The Lights return to normal as they stand and bow deeply. Their supporters lead the applause*

Maid What the dickens was that all about?

Jam 2 Well, I wouldn't expect you to understand.

Maid And where did the blinkin' melons come in?

Jam 2 The melons were symbolic. Obviously.

Maid But where were they? There weren't no melons!

Jam 1 If you read your programme notes you'll see that the whole piece takes place *within* a rotting melon.

Vicar Oh, yes, of course. That makes complete sense.

Spinster I din't see no rottin' melons. They can't get points for set when there ain't no rottin' melon...

Jam 3 You use your imagination. If you've got one.

Ted (*separating them*) Yes, yes. Keep your hair on. And the score for Frantic Jam—eight out of ten!

Frantic Jam (*triumphantly*) Yes!

Vicar Eight out of ten? And no set? They only got eight because she groped you.

Ted Not at all. I found the whole piece very stirring...

Spinster Yes, I'm sure you did.

Ted ...and that's my professional opinion; so it's first blood to Frantic Jam!

Frantic Jam (*chanting and pointing*) One—nil! One—nil! One—nil!

Ted Right! Let's see what the same group make of that scene from *A Killing at the Parsonage.*

The miserable stage manager brings on scripts

As Frantic Jam look through the scripts...

Jam 3 (*to Bletchworth, snapping her fingers*) The tape.

Spinster What?

Jam 3 We need your silly music if we're going to do your silly play.

Maid Use your own blinkin' music, shorty.

The Lights dip and the weird music returns. The red and green lights come up again as Frantic Jam take up their bizarre positions, this time to perform the scene from A Killing at the Parsonage. *Jam 1 plays the Vicar, Jam 3 the Maid and Jam 2 the Spinster. If there are other Jams, they may writhe in and out of those with speaking parts. They perform it as they did their own piece—with strange movement and expression and coarse accents. As the weird music fades...*

Jam 3 Oh! Bless me, Vicar, I din't see you there!

Jam 1 (*miming eyes on stalks*) You're looking in fine fettle today, Jasmine.

Jam 3 Oh, sir, you must not be so familiar. (*She mimes shunning him*) Miss Littlewood, the mistress of the 'ouse, may come upon us at any moment.

Jam 1 I don't care, I tell you.

Jam 3 But surely you remember that you are engaged to Miss Littlewood and that she is a woman who, though 'andsome and much-admired, 'as saved 'erself for the time when you can be married?

Jam 1 Yes, Jasmine, I know. Oh, curse the day I allowed her to play fast and loose with my unknowing 'eart! (*He mimes a pounding heart*)

Jam 3 But for the objection of 'er brother, Colonel Littlewood, late of India, you would be married even now.

Jam 1 Yes, yes. And yet if we married, the Colonel would cut 'er out of 'is will... (*he mimes scissors*) ...because of 'is strange aversion to clergymen. We would be penniless.

Jam 3 I am already penniless, 'Ector.

Jam 1 Oh, Jasmine! If only the Littlewoods would disappear, leaving their wealth behind, then you and I...

Jam 3 We are trapped, 'Ector.

Jam 1 Trapped, Jasmine!

They all mime being trapped in a glass box, chanting, "Trapped, trapped!"

Spinster Garbage! Complete garbage! There's no line in our play about being trapped!

Ted (*dancing forward*) Keep to the script, keep to the script! (*He counts them out*) One ... two ... three...

Jam 1 and 3 go straight into a stylised clinch

Jam 2 enters and mimes terrible shock

Jam 2 'Ector! What is the meaning of this?

Jam 1 Things are not as they seem, 'Enrietta. Your brother, the Colonel, asked me to speak to your maid 'ere, to comfort 'er in 'er sadness...

Jam 2 Indeed?

Jam 3 (*miming sadness*) Yes, ma'am. Begging your pardon, ma'am. The Vicar was consoling me. You see, my poor aunt has gorn down with the lumbago.

They all crook their backs

Jam 2 I am not at all convinced by this talk of lumbago. (*She breaks off. In own voice*) You can say that again. (*She resumes*) But I cannot deal with this now. I 'ave just come from the conservatory. The Colonel is ... is...

Vicar Another extra bit! They're cockin' up an extremely fine play 'ere!

Jam 2 Shut your face! (*She resumes*) The Colonel is ... dead!

They all strike a dramatic attitude of shock and horror. The red and green lights fade, the weird music is back for a moment. Return to normal lighting and they bow deeply. Applause, led heartily by their supporters. The miserable stage manager collects scripts and begins to hand out others to Bletchworth

Ted Thank you, thank you. Though I wasn't convinced that you entirely captured the spirit of the thing. And your music didn't quite say "English Country Parsonage" to me.

Spinster It said "acute diarrhoea" to me.

Jam 3 The rat-bags wouldn't let us use their tape!

Ted Also, you have to remember what I've been saying all week——

Pause. Everyone looks blank. They obviously haven't been taking notice and Ted is hurt

Sub-text! Sub-text, sub-text, sub-text! (*Beat*) And levels. Where were your levels?

Jam 1 What are you talking about, levels? How can you use levels in crap like that?

Ted You could've used a ladder or something. Anyway, well done, but not quite *there* somehow. Six out of ten.

Bletchworth Yes! (*They break into song*) If you're useless and you know it, clap your 'ands! (*Etc.*)

Jam 2 Oh, yes? Well, you haven't done our scene yet. Let's see who's laughing then.

Iris Yes, tell them to get on with it, for pity's sake.

Ted Right. Ladies and gentlemen, we now present The Bletchworth Players in a scene from *To Make Do With Melons*.

The Lights dip and the jolly English music plays. As it fades, and the bright lights and birdsong of the garden return, Bletchworth come forward and take up rather wooden and embarrassed positions. Pause

Spinster Just a minute. We need the cymbal. (*She breaks out of the group and goes over to Frantic Jam*) Let's 'ave a lend of your cymbal...

Jam 2 You must be joking. You wouldn't let us have your tape so you're not having our cymbal.

Vicar But that ain't fair.

Jam 2 Tough bananas. You'll have to mime.

The Spinster returns and strikes an imaginary cymbal. Nothing happens

Spinster Start, then.

Maid I din't hear nothin'.

Spinster Course you din't. Those mean beggars won't let me use their cymbal.

Vicar Then you'll have to make the noise, otherwise we won't know when to start.

Spinster But I can't...

Vicar Just do it, you daft sow!

Spinster (*half-heartedly*) Bong.

Jam 1 Pathetic.

Vicar (*half-heartedly*) The rats are gnawing at the skirting board!

Bletchworth The rats. The rats.

Spinster Bong-bong-bong-ong-ong.

They begin to walk awkwardly about

Jam 2 Good grief! They're so wooden!

Jam 1 Absolutely! Wood, wood, wood.

Jam 3 Complete planks.

Ted Please! Leave the criticism to me, if you don't mind.

Spinster (*to Ted*) Thank you. (*She resumes*) Father of rats, speak to us. Leave the broken bedstead and the curled remains of last night's sandwiches. The blood of the questing rat has entered our veins.

Maid We scuttle in shadows.

Bletchworth Scuttle, scuttle, scuttle...

They walk backwards and forwards a few steps

Vicar We scavenge and seek.

Bletchworth We become rats in your name.

A pretend bang on the cymbal. They walk stiffly about again

The blood of the rat. The blood of the rat. (*Etc.*)

The Maid moves over to Ted and runs her fingers through his hair and over his chest. She outdoes Jam 3

Maid The blood of the rat courses through my veins. (*In her own voice*) And I'll do anythin', practically *anythin'* once I get rat blood in me veins.

Jam 1 I say!

Spinster But wait. I have just come from the conservatory and the Father of Rats is ... is ... dead!

They strike their familiar, dramatic poses—the Maid faints, the Vicar catches her, etc.

Jam 2 No, he is not dead! You can't say that...

Maid Yes, we can. You changed our play...

Jam 2 But the Father of Rats simply can't die like that.

Maid 'E can. 'E et a bit of poisoned melon.

The Spinster provides a pretend rolling note on the cymbal. Bletchworth walk C *and form a huddle. Pause*

Ted Have you done?

Vicar Not quite. (*To the others*) Wait 'ere. Don't move.

Vicar walks off and returns with a step-ladder, which he sets up and then climbs

They strike another pose. The Lights dip and the English music plays. When the Lights return to normal, they stand and bow deeply. Their supporters lead the applause

Ted (*clapping*) Well done, Bletchworth, well done. Perhaps it lacked the fluidity that this script demanded, but you did make excellent use of levels, so I award you seven out of ten.

Bletchworth (*chanting and pointing*) One—all! One—all! One—all!

Iris You mean it's still a dead-heat?

Ted Yes, I'm afraid so. One round each.

Iris You stupid git. We're no further forward.

Vicar Yes, we are. Add up the points. Fourteen to them and fourteen

and an 'alf to us. (*He snatches the trophy*) Thank you very
much...

Jam 1 Hang on, hang on. You were deducted half a point for
interrupting.

Vicar Don't be daft. You interrupted, too.

Ted No, no. They're right. The scores are still the same.

Uproar, quelled by Iris

Iris Calm down, all of you! There's still nothing between the teams,
so we must go into the tie-breaker.

Jam 3 And what's that?

Iris The Dramatic Sprint.

Vicar The what?

Iris The Dramatic Sprint. It's in the BOGOFF rules and it's
perfectly simple. Each group performs the same speech at the
same time. The one who gets through it first wins. And we can all
go home.

Spinster Utter cobblers!

There is an uproar of protest from both groups

Iris (*bellowing to quell them*) Order! Order! Compose yourselves,
please!

The uproar dies

Thank you. I've had just about all I can stand of this posturing
nonsense from both teams.

Ted Quite right.

Iris And complete spineless indecision from you.

Ted I say.

Iris Will you remember that you are actors and should conduct
yourselves with decorum? Either you do the Dramatic Sprint or
you'll both be disqualified.

They hang their heads

Well?

Jam 2 We're not giving up now; we'll do it.

Maid And so will we. What's it to be?

Iris To be, or not to be...

Maid That's what I say. What's it to be?

Iris ...that is the question.

Maid I know it's the question, woman. What's the bloomin' answer?

Jam 1 It's Shakespeare, you prune. Though I don't suppose you've ever done Shakespeare.

Vicar We 'ave! We 'ave! We done *The Midsummer Night's Murders!*

Jam 1 Dream.

Vicar Dream. That's what I said. I was what's-'is-name... Ron something or other...

Jam 1 Oberon.

Vicar All right, smart-arse. I know what I was!

Ted For heaven's sake! Don't start all that again...

Jam 2 Just one moment. Please. We are artists. We live for our work. This is a *Drama* Festival? A celebration of the *Arts*? And you expect us to spout the Bard? At speed?

Iris If you want to win the Festival, yes.

Jam 2 Right. Then let's get on with it.

Iris Thank you. So get to your places and prepare for the off. Then we can all go home.

The two groups line up across the stage for the start. They do limbering-up exercises, as sprinters might

Ted Are you ready, teams?

The teams tense themselves

On your marks! Get set! Go!

Both teams launch into the speech. There is a great deal of shouting,

*cheering and jeering during this. They don't get through the speech,
though, because after a few lines the teams start nudging each other.
The nudges become shoves and the shoves develop into full-blown
fisticuffs*

Both teams   To be, or not to be—that is the question:
                  Whether 'tis nobler in the mind to suffer
                  The slings and arrows of outrageous fortune
                  Or to take arms against a sea of troubles,
                  And by opposing end 'em. To die—to sleep——
                  No more; and by a sleep to say we end
                  The 'eartache, and the thousand natural shocks
                  That flesh is heir to. 'Tis a consummation
                  Devoutly to be wish'd. To die—to sleep.
                  To sleep—perchance to dream: ay, there's the rub!
                  For in that sleep of death what dreams may come
                  When we have shuffled off this mortal coil,
                  Must give us pause.

The writhing mob is in full flow when the Vicar breaks away

Vicar (*shouting*) Please! Stop all this fightin'! Please! What 'as
become of us? What are we doin'? Stop it, please!

*Gradually the fight stops, except for Ted and Iris who have launched
into a fight of their own. They continue into the silence left by the
others*

Iris You buffoon! You've made a complete mockery of my
festival!
Ted Bed and breakfast, you said. And what did I get? A mattress
in a shed!
Iris It's not a shed—it's an extension!
Ted A doss-house!

*Iris is about to clobber him with his clipboard when they become
aware that everyone else is watching them. They withdraw, smiling*

Vicar Thank you. This is all wrong. I feel... I feel so ashamed of
meself. Because this is not what we've come for. All those hours
of rehearsal and study—it weren't meant to end like this. But I
allowed meself to be tempted by the lure of trophies. And, blimey,
we din't come 'ere just for trophies, just to score points, did we?
Maid Yes, we did.
Vicar No. No, we din't. Points and trophies—what do they mean?
They mean nothin' set against the *real* reason for being 'ere. (*To
the Maid*) Listen, I'm sorry I called you a dozy cow. That's not
what I feel, not what I feel at all. I value your friendship, and yet
I called my friend a dozy cow just because she forgot a line. (*To
the others*) Are we not *all* friends 'ere? Friends united in the cause
of theatre. Which is bigger than any of us, really.

*The teams are subdued by this. Some look disgruntled, but others
mutter a few words of approval*

Can I tell you something? Something I've never told no-one
before? Just bein' 'ere, on this stage and in this company, means
the world to me. Can I share that with you? You see, I'm not a very
confident person.

Murmurs of dissent

No, I find it 'ard ... to express meself. And yet to act *is* to express
meself. The theatre 'as given me a voice. (*He wipes a tear from
his eye*) And if I'm honest I've learned somethin' tonight. (*He
gestures at Frantic Jam*) Seeing these wonderful performers 'as
opened me eyes. I've seen grace and skill in what you done, my
friends, my very dear friends. You 'ave taught me a new way, and
I shall always be grateful to you for that.

Frantic Jam has gradually been won over by this

Jam 2 Don't mention it. It was a pleasure, wasn't it?

The Jam contingent call out in agreement

Vicar We're comrades really, ain't we? Mates. Brothers and
sisters. That's what it's actually about. I'd like to thank you for
that. (*He claps Frantic Jam*)

*The others join in and Frantic Jam hang their heads modestly.
Frantic Jam and Bletchworth are now at peace. Some are hand in
hand, some arm in arm, etc.*

So, what I'm really sayin' is I already feel like a winner because
I 'ave gained new friends. I don't know about the rest of you, but
that's more than enough for me. In fact, what I'd like to do now
is to shake each one of you by the 'and, and give you my 'eartfelt
thanks, and say to you: please, take the trophy...

A small gasp from the others

It's yours by rights. You were wonderful and it belongs to you. I
concede!
Spinster Yes, yes! We concede!
Maid The trophy should go to the best group, and the best group is
Frantic Jam!
Jam 3 No, no. You were better than us. Your play was really
moving, you know.

Frantic Jam call out their agreement

Vicar We 'ad our moments—I ain't gonna deny it—but you were
fresh and original. And the trophy's yours!
Jam 1 Thank you, thank you. (*He clasps the Vicar's hand*)

They embrace tearfully. Ted, moved to tears, comes forward

Ted Ladies and gentlemen, this young man has, I think, spoken for
us all.

Shouts of assent

And, I think you'll all agree, he has spoken most articulately and from the depths of his being in a fashion I shall long remember. Ladies and gentlemen, fellow theatre-lovers, I feel I should mark this rather special moment in the only way I know how. By awarding him an extra point!

Frantic Jam Hear, hear!

Iris An extra point? But surely, that means…

Vicar I think we all know what it means, Iris. It means that our adjudicator is a true 'uman being with a good 'eart.

Applause for Ted

But it means somethin' else, too, don't it? It means we've won. (*A great triumphant gesture*) Yes! We've done it! We've won!

Suddenly Bletchworth and their supporters celebrate and cheer. The Vicar grabs the trophy

Jam 1 You cheat. You dirty, rotten low-down cheat.

Vicar (*to Frantic Jam*) Eat dirt, you scumbags! There's only one winner in this game and it ain't you!

The Vicar runs off with the trophy and the others pursue him round the stage. They all end up c in a huge scrum. In the tangle, Iris has got possession of the trophy (though of course, no-one sees her do this). Suddenly, the Vicar raises his hands above the mêlée and finds them empty. All freeze, staring at his empty hands. There is a moment's sudden silence. As the music comes up, Iris emerges from the scrum with the trophy and begins to tiptoe off with it

CURTAIN

FURNITURE AND PROPERTY LIST

Further dressing may be added at the director's discretion

On stage: Clipboard
Table. *On it*: large white cloth bearing the legend "BOGOFF",
large tasteless trophy, several tiny trophies, jug of water,
glass
Cymbal

Off stage: Scripts (**SM**)
Step-ladder (**Vicar**)

LIGHTING PLOT

Property fittings required: nil
1 interior. The same throughout

| *Cue* 1 | **Vicar** and **Spinster** exit | (Page 5) |
| | *Fade lights down* | |

| *Cue* 2 | **Maid** moves c | (Page 5) |
| | *Bring up bright lighting* | |

| *Cue* 3 | **Maid** faints and **Vicar** catches her | (Page 8) |
| | *Fade lights down* | |

| *Cue* 4 | Jolly English music comes up | (Page 8) |
| | *Bring up normal lighting* | |

| *Cue* 5 | **SM** returns and makes some signals | (Page 8) |
| | *Fade lights down* | |

| *Cue* 6 | Music fades | (Page 8) |
| | *Bring up red and green lights (possibly throbbing)* | |

| *Cue* 7 | **All** run c and form an artistic huddle | (Page 10) |
| | *After a pause, fade red and green lights* | |

| *Cue* 8 | Weird music comes up, then ends | (Page 10) |
| | *Bring up normal lighting* | |

| *Cue* 9 | **Maid**: "Use your own blinkin' music, shorty." | (Page 11) |
| | *Fade lights down* | |

Cue 10   Weird music returns   (Page 11)
              Bring up red and green lights

Cue 11   **All** strike dramatic attitude of shock   (Page 12)
              Fade red and green lights

Cue 12   Weird music is back for a moment   (Page 12)
              Bring up normal lighting

Cue 13   **Ted**: "...from *To Make Do With Melons*."   (Page 13)
              Fade lights down

Cue 14   Jolly English music plays, then fades   (Page 13)
              Bring up bright lighting

Cue 15   **All** strike another pose   (Page 15)
              Fade lights down

Cue 16   English music plays   (Page 15)
              Bring up normal lighting

EFFECTS PLOT

Cue 1	Lights dip *Music: something tuneful and jolly English*	(Page 5)
Cue 2	Lights come up brightly *Birdsong*	(Page 6)
Cue 3	Lights fade *Jolly English music*	(Page 8)
Cue 4	Lights go down *Weird electronic music, then fade*	(Page 8)
Cue 5	Red and green lights fade *Weird music, then fade*	(Page 10)
Cue 6	Lights dip *Weird music*	(Page 11)
Cue 7	**Frantic Jam** start performing *Fade weird music*	(Page 11)
Cue 8	Red and green lights fade *Weird music for a moment*	(Page 12)
Cue 9	Lights dip *Jolly English music, then fade*	(Page 13)
Cue 10	Bright lights come up *Birdsong*	(Page 13)

Cue 11   Lights dip   (Page 15)
            English music

Cue 12   **All** freeze in silence   (Page 21)
            Music

Lightning Source UK Ltd.
Milton Keynes UK
UKOW01f1102240715

255765UK00001B/22/P